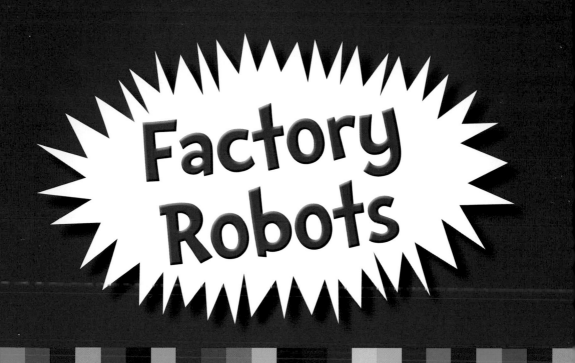

# Factory Robots

BY NADIA HIGGINS

AMICUS HIGH INTEREST • AMICUS INK

Amicus High Interest and Amicus Ink are imprints of Amicus
P.O. Box 1329, Mankato, MN 56002
www.amicuspublishing.us

Library of Congress Cataloging-in-Publication Data
Names: Higgins, Nadia, author.
Title: Factory robots / by Nadia Higgins.
Description: Mankato, Minnesota : Amicus High Interest, 2018.
  | Series:  Robotics in our world | Includes index.
Identifiers: LCCN 2016034047 (print) | LCCN 2016035919
  (ebook) | ISBN 9781681511412 (library binding) | ISBN
  9781681521725 (pbk.) | ISBN 9781681512310 (ebook)
  | ISBN 9781681512310 (pdf)
Subjects:  LCSH: Robots, Industrial–Juvenile literature.
Classification: LCC TS191.8 .H54 2018 (print) | LCC TS191.8
  (ebook) | DDC  629.8/92–dc23
LC record available at https://lccn.loc.gov/2016034047

Editor: Wendy Dieker
Series Designer: Kathleen Petelinsek
Book Designer: Tracy Myers
Photo Researcher: Holly Young

Photo Credits: Factory_Easy/Shutterstock cover; Andrei
Kholmov/shutterstock 4-5; Wirapong Samlee /123rf 6;
asharkyu/shutterstock 9, 14-15, 17, 18; Photoquest/Getty
Images/Getty/10; UL Digital Library/WikiCommons 13; A.
Farnsworth/SuperStock 21; Courtesy of Rethink Robotics, Inc./
Rethink Robotics Press Kit 22-23; Dragan Trifunovic/iStock 25;
Eliza Grinnell/Harvard/Flickr 26; ndoeljindoel/shutterstock/29

Printed in the United States of America

HC 10 9 8 7 6 5 4 3 2 1
PB 10 9 8 7 6 5 4 3 2 1

# Table of Contents

# Robot Builders

In the car factory, motors roar. Sparks fly. Stinky smoke fills the air. But the workers do not mind at all. They are robots! Twelve robot arms are building a car frame. Big arms pick up heavy sheets of metal. The metal seems as light as paper to them. The robots put the pieces in place.

Robots help build cars in a factory. They do some of the dangerous parts of the job.

Smaller robot arms swoop in. They **weld** the metal sheets together. In just three minutes, the car's body is done. The robots do not take a break. They begin on a new car. On and on they go. Factory robots make just about every car on the road.

**Sparks fly as a robot welds metal together on a car frame.**

Robots also make ovens and computers. They help pack and ship things. Robots help with pencils, socks, noodles, and more! Most of your stuff has been touched by a robot.

A machine can do just one job. But a robot can do many jobs in a row. In a factory, robots do dangerous or boring jobs that people used to do.

 How many robots work in factories around the world?

**Robots can put very small parts together better than a person can.**

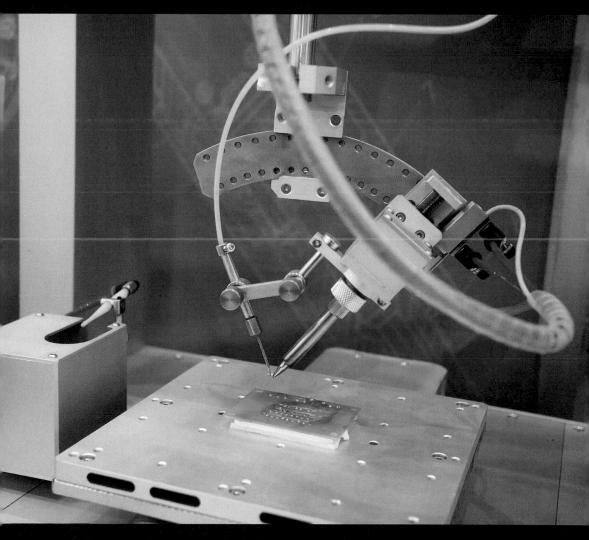

 More than 1 million.

# The Rise of Robots

In the 1700s, people wanted to build lots of things as quickly as possible. **Fabric mills** popped up around the U.S. By the late 1800s, factories made cars, candy, and other things.

In 1913, Henry Ford started building cars on an **assembly line**. Each worker did one small job as a car moved along. These workers got bored.

Each worker at the Ford plant did one small, boring job all day.

Fast forward to the 1950s. Along came computers and robots. In 1961, the first factory robot arrived. It worked in a car plant in New Jersey. A computer told the robot what to do. The Unimate robot arm could lift 500 pounds (226 kg). It could stack hot sheets of metal all day long. People no longer had to do hard and boring jobs.

A worker sets up a Unimate PUMA robot in a factory in 1986.

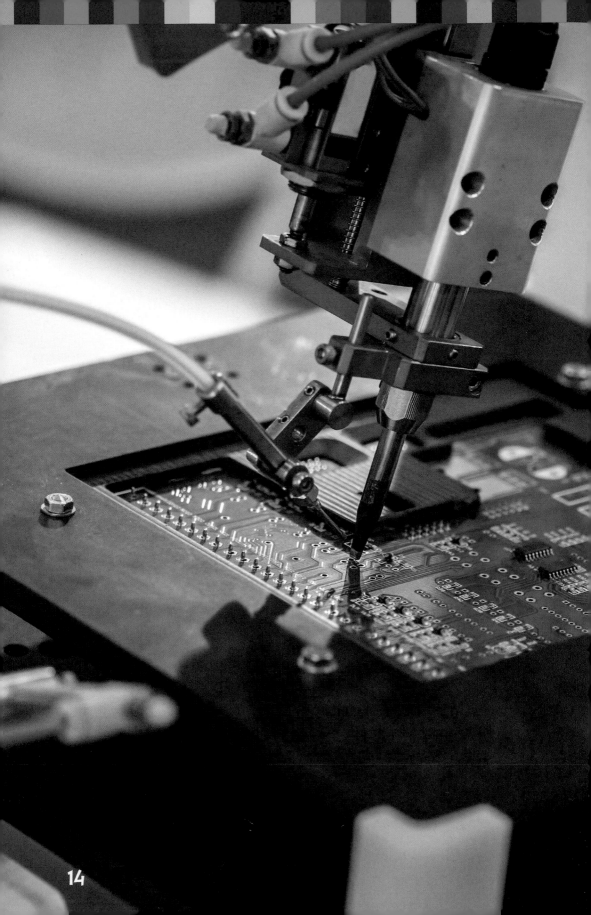

Factory owners were amazed. Robots were so strong and fast. They barely ever made mistakes. And they did not need lunch breaks. As time went on, robots got cheaper. They became easier to use. They moved in new ways. And they were so precise. A robot could do work too fine for human hands.

A robot builds tiny circuit boards for electronics.

# How Do Factory Robots Work?

A factory robot is usually a big arm. It has three main parts. The computer is like the robot's brain. It tells the arm how to move. The **drive system** is like the muscles. Often, motors make up this part. They power the arm so it can lift and bend. The **effectors** are like hands. They are the tools that do the work.

 How many hands does a robot have?

**Robots in factories are usually an arm that moves. A hand is at the end.**

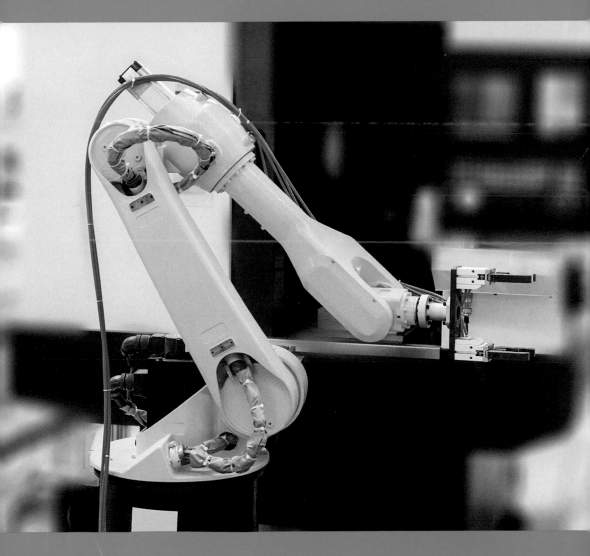

 It could have several. One hand may be a claw or a sprayer. It could be a brush or drill. These parts can go on and come off.

**A robot hand gently works dough into a twist donut.**

 **Q** Can a robot sense things that humans cannot?

Many robots have **sensors**. These are like the robot's eyes, ears, and skin. A camera lets a robot see. The robot can pick out the right candy to put in a box. A microphone lets a robot hear. You can tell it what to do. Some robots can feel **pressure**. They can pick up a cookie without breaking it.

Yes. For example, some robots can tell if a magnet is near.

How do robots know what to do? A person **programs** the robot's computer. That tells the robot exactly how to move. Sometimes the operator may show the robot instead. The person moves the arm with a remote control. Next time, the robot will move by itself.

Do factory robots keep us safe?

A worker watches the robot arms in a car factory.

Yes and no. Robots do dangerous jobs. But swinging robot arms are no joke! Most robots work behind fences.

# Future Robots

Almost all factory robots do one simple job. But small factories don't have room for hundreds of robots each doing one job. These places need robots that can do many jobs. Meet Baxter. This robot has a head, arms, and legs. Anybody can teach it a job. They just move its body, like a dance partner!

Baxter the robot can do a different job every day.

All robots are machines. They need a power source. Some are plugged in to the wall. Others have batteries that need to be replaced or charged up. One day, robots may run on sunlight. Or they will use garbage to make energy. They will not need cords or chargers. Scientists keep working on better ways to power robots.

 What do you call a person who invents new robots?

**Robots would move more freely if they didn't have to be plugged in.**

 He or she is a roboticist.

These small robots sense the next step of the job. They work together to create a structure.

Imagine a swarm of termites building a mound. Each little bug has a job. Scientists wondered if tiny robots could work this way too. Small robots called TERMES can work together to make a building. Each robot is programed with the final plans. Then it senses what is around. It figures out what step is next. Little by little, each tiny robot works to get a big job done.

# Looking Ahead

Robots break down. They need to be fixed. Robots can already help with this problem. They send messages to their human helpers. "Check me." Or, "I need oil." They still need people. But what if robots could just fix themselves? What if robots could build other robots? That idea makes some people shiver with fear. It makes other people squirm with excitement. How about you?

 Are any robots as smart as people?

**A robot is still just a machine. It needs a person to fix it.**

 Not yet. Robots still have trouble with many basic human skills. For example, a robot cannot tell the difference between a doll and a real baby.

29

# Glossary

**assembly line** A way of building things, where work passes from one worker to the next until the job is complete.

**drive system** The system of parts on a robot that make it move.

**effector** The part on a robot that does a job; it is like the robot's "hand."

**fabric mill** A factory that makes cotton, wool, or other materials into fabric for clothing, furniture, and other goods.

**pressure** The feeling of something pushing against your skin.

**program** To give instructions to a computer.

**sensor** A robot part that allows the robot to sense light, pressure, or sound.

**weld** To melt pieces of metal so they stick together.

# Read More

**Cassriel, Betsy R.** *Robot Builders!* Broomall, Penn: Mason Crest, 2016.

**Ceceri, Kathy.** *Making Simple Robots: Exploring Cutting-Edge Robotics with Everyday Stuff.* Sebastopol, Cal: Maker Media, 2015.

**Shulman, Mark and James Buckley Jr.** *Time for Kids Explorers: Robots.* New York: Time Home Entertainment Inc., 2014.

# Websites

**The Big Picture: Robots**
*http://archive.boston.com/bigpicture/2009/03/robots.html*

**Challenge: Robots!**
*http://education.nationalgeographic.org/game/challenge-robots/*

**Robotics: Facts**
*http://idahoptv.org/sciencetrek/topics/robots/facts.cfm*

# Index

# About the Author

Nadia Higgins is the author of more than 100 books for children and young adults. She has written about everything from ants to zombies, with many science and technology topics in between. Higgins lives in Minneapolis, Minnesota, with her human family, pet lizard, and robotic dog.